advance praise for
Open My Lips

Rachel Barenblat has achieved a remarkable feat with her latest collection.
Kristin Berkey-Abbott, author of *Whistling Past the Graveyard* and *I Stand Here Shredding Documents*

Rabbi Barenblat's poems are like those rare cover songs that bring new insights to familiar rhythms and melodies. Her interpretations of ancient liturgy turn up the volume and realign the balance on our tradition's greatest hits.
Rabbi Elana Zelony, Congregation Beth Shalom, San Francisco

"You enfold me in this bathtowel/You enliven me with coffee," writes Barenblat in OPEN MY LIPS, a collection of accessible and compelling prayer-poems that manages to locate the sacred in the quotidian. After reading these poems, one realizes the ordinary moment is filled with hidden light, and inspiration isn't as far away as we often assume.
Yehoshua November, author of *God's Optimism*

Barenblat's God is a personal God—one who lets her cry on His shoulder, and who rocks her like a colicky baby. These poems bridge the gap between the ineffable and the human. This collection will bring comfort to those with a religion of their own, as well as those seeking a relationship with some kind of higher power.
Satya Robyn, author of *The Most Beautiful Thing and Thaw*

Rachel Barenblat's latest offering is truly beautiful— moving, ethereal, grounded, accessible and profound.
Rabbi Wendi Geffen, North Shore Congregation Israel, Chicago

Incredibly moving. She opens a path for the reader to feel and understand the traditional Jewish liturgy from a modern feminine perspective. I love it!

Rabbi Rebecca Sirbu, director, Rabbis Without Borders

Her project is to find the sacred in every moment, high or low, and to turn towards it without hesitation. Her lesson for us is larger than the lesson of any particular ritual of any particular tradition: that if we have not yet found the sacred meaning of any thing, we have not yet looked hard enough.

Dale Favier, author of *Opening the World*

Praise for Rachel Barenblat's previous works

Her poems have the classic cadence of the scriptures and the fresh wonder of a new mother. These are old words for the modern mind. This is ancient wisdom we can feel and know.

Pastor Gordon Atkinson, author of *RealLivePreacher.com*

These poems are so out there, so radical, and at the same time so gentle and inviting. Barenblat manages to do work that has passion and truth behind it, without ranting.

Alicia Ostriker, author of *For the Love of God: the Bible as an Open Book* and *The Book of Seventy*

These rich poems will carry you into the great timeless miracle and mystery of unfolding littleness, nonstop maternal alertness, beauty and exhaustion and amazing, exquisite tenderness, oh yes.

Naomi Shihab Nye, author of *Fuel* and *The Words Under the Words*

Rachel Barenblat's poems are easy to enter into, and they carry both the uniqueness of her persona as poet and serious Jew and the universality of love that has made us all.

Rodger Kamenetz, author of *The Jew in the Lotus*

Open My Lips

prayers and poems

Rachel Barenblat

Ben Yehuda Press
Teaneck, New Jersey

Published by Ben Yehuda Press
122 Ayers Court 1#B
Teaneck, NJ 07666

http://www.BenYehudaPress.com

ISBN13 978-1-934730-48-5

Library of Congress Cataloging-in-Publication Data

Names: Barenblat, Rachel Evelyne, -1975 author.
Title: Open my lips : prayers and poems / Rachel Barenblat.
Description: Teaneck, NJ : Ben Yehuda Press, [2016" | [2016
Identifiers: LCCN 2016006238 | ISBN 9781934730485
Subjects: LCSH: Judaism--Prayers and devotions.
Classification: LCC BM665.A2 B2016 37 | DDC --5/296.4 dc23
LC record available at http://lccn.loc.gov/2016006238

19 18 17 16 / 10 9 8 7 6 5 4 3 2 1   20160317

Also by Rachel Barenblat

70 faces: Torah poems
Waiting to Unfold

the skies here
What Stays
chaplainbook
Through
See Me: Elul poems
Toward Sinai: Omer poems

for my teachers

and my students

and for the students of my students

Contents

What is prayer?

In the Jewish understanding, prayer is an opportunity to offer gratitude for our blessings, to connect with something greater than ourselves, to link ourselves with ancestors and with community, to reach toward meaning. The Hebrew word להתפלל / *l'hitpallel*, "to pray," connotes self-examination. Through prayer, we discern the subtle ebbs and flows of heart and soul.

Prayer is one form of the spiritual work, or service, which we do to build and strengthen our connection with something beyond ourselves, which we usually name as God.

A traditional Jewish prayerbook contains poetry and prose written over the course of millennia. Hebrew prayer is inestimably rich and deep. But I know it isn't always accessible to those who don't have the time or inclination to master Hebrew.

This book stands at the intersection of contemporary poetry. and Jewish liturgy, my two lifelong loves. It aims to bridge some of the distance between you (the pray-er) and Jewish prayer as a practice. And you don't need to know a word of Hebrew in order to dive in.

Here are prayers that double as poems and poems that double as psalms: for daily use, for weekly use, for use around the wheel of the Jewish year, for use in times of sorrow or struggle, for thanksgiving and consolation. And though these prayers are written from a Jewish standpoint, I hope they will also speak to people of other faith-traditions, and to those who affiliate with no tradition at all.

In Psalms 69:14, we read וַאֲנִי תְפִלָּתִי-לְךָ יְהוָה, עֵת רָצוֹן / Va'ani tefilati l'kha HaShem eit ratzon. "As for me, my prayer is to You, God, in a time of yearning." Some choose to creatively translate this as "And I: I am my prayer..." May these prayers help you to open your lips and unlock the vault of your heart and to make your very self into a prayer, stretching into the beyond.

Rabbi Rachel Barenblat
2016 / 5776

Daily Prayer

Elohai Neshama: **My soul is pure**

My God, my
own: my soul
that You have given me
is pure, clear
like mikvah waters

the spark
which makes me more
than automated clay,
than cells sprouting cells
is holy

neshama: feminine
no matter whose,
women and men
and those blessed
in-between

what's gendered
female is what
creates: this
drop of divine
breath that breathes in us

let what I create
in the world, my God,
be as pure
as Your breath
in me

Asher Yatzar: You Who created my body

Blessed is the breath of life
who formed and animates this body,

its myriad organs and tissues,
protrusions, bones, and sinews;

winter skin so dry my calves rub bloody,
flesh flushed with rhythm and heat;

curve of hip distinguishing me
from my mother whose pants need belting;

nailbeds a reincarnation
of my grandmother's long fingers;

tiny dunes of bicep I have labored
to bring into being and maintain;

narrow feet which fit snug
only in the most expensive of shoes;

wrists and ankles I can encircle
with thumb and forefinger;

nose and mouth that together savor
cheese, real vanilla, green tea;

all the weird, wet, noisy orifices
I need daily but can't understand.

If my bowels were to fail, or my kidneys,
pancreas, vision...? Doctors would stitch and sew,

Rachel Barenblat

but it wouldn't be easy
and You'd still have to prop me up

as You do today and every day.
Blessed are You, creator of embodied miracles.

Baruch She'amar: **Blessed is the One who speaks**

Every sunrise and sunset, birth
and death, storm and flood, blossom
and snowfall. Every lip balm,
paperback novel, beggar and bowl
and hair salon. Every glass of water,
muddy gorge, mother
and market and corrugated roof.

Rhododendrons, dirty oil barrels
filled with groundnut paste,
filligreed teapots, emerald beetles,
scrolls, wooden tulips, bottles of beer.
Sequoias, crepe myrtle, dwarf birch.
Every rubber band. Every paperclip.
Every open sore and aching tooth.

How does Your mouth not tire
of speaking the world into being?
Almighty, Your creations cannot imagine
infinity without growing weary.
It's hard to remember
Your mouth is purely metaphor
though Your speech is real.

You speak every atom in the universe,
a mighty chord resonating.
Every fold of skin, every grain of sand,
every iceberg and hibiscus comes from you.
If You ever chose silence, even for an instant,
we would blink out of existence
as though this experiment had never been.

Rachel Barenblat

Morning Prayer

Some days I say good morning
while the hose splashes into the kiddie pool
and the cat sniffs curiously at its curls

my lightest tallit
a sweep of blue silk
across bare shoulders

Blessed are You
Who straightens the bent, I sing
as I reach for the heavens

and blessed is the One
Who speaks creation into being,
walking across a patch of wild thyme

the mosquitoes want to rejoice in me
so I swish my *tzitzit*
inscribing letters on the air

then swirl my tallit off
like a bullfighter's cloak
blue rippling around my fingers

it's time to go inside
I turn off the faucet
but Your abundance keeps flowing

Daily Miracles

You bring my son's footfalls to my door
and shock me awake with his cold heels against my ribs.

You teach me to distinguish waking life from dreaming.
You press the wooden floor against the soles of my feet.

You slip my eyeglasses into my questing hand
and the world comes into focus again.

In the time before time You collected hydrogen and oxygen
into molecules which stream now from my showerhead.

You enfold me in this bathtowel.
You enliven me with coffee.

Every morning you remake me in your image
and free me to push back against my fears.

You are the balance that holds up my spine,
the light in my gritty, grateful eyes.

Rachel Barenblat

Tele/Presence

I want to keep You with me
when I raise the remote
turn the dial, flick the knob

when I fall to the temptation
of reading the comments
at *Ha'aretz* or the *Post*

I want Your presence
twined around my forearm
when I snap open the Times

when I fret over trending topics
when I dream in status updates
scrolling endlessly

remind me, God, to seek You
not only in the timeless flow
of liturgy on the page

but in the stock ticker
and the commercials for windshields
and the interplay of punditry

beyond the debt ceiling
within every celebrity
there is nothing but You

Without Ceasing

The wash of dawn across the sky
reveals Your signature.

Cicadas drone Your praise
through the honey-slow afternoon.

The angular windmills on the ridge
recite Your name with every turn.

And I, who can barely focus on breath
without drifting into story:

what can I say to You,
author of wisteria and sorrel,

You who shaped these soft hills
with glaciers' slow passage?

You fashioned me as a gong:
your presence reverberates.

Help me to open my lips
that I may sing Your praise.

Rachel Barenblat

Elul and the Days of Awe

Rocking chair (for Elul)

The exalted throne on high
  is a gliding rocker.
    God watches us with kind eyes

rejoicing when we figure out
  how to fit two pieces together
    and create something new

looking on us with compassion
  when we struggle for balance
    and thirst for what we can't name.

The sages of the Talmud knew
  more than the wobbly calf wants to suck
    the mother yearns to give milk

God is the same way
  overflowing with blessings, and yet
    we turn our faces away and wail.

When will we learn?
  God's lap is always open
    all we have to do is return.

Aspiration (for Elul)

What matters isn't
who I am on retreat,
singing the day into being,

but who I am
when I've come home
to the cat and the bills,

to-do list as long
as the yoga mat
I too rarely unfurl.

The real work
is living my intentions
at my desk, the laptop open;

in a slow-moving line
at the grocery store
past screaming tabloids;

when someone I love
loses a job or a partner
or a body that works.

Elul, this moon
cycling its phases
before the days of awe

is a string on my finger
tefillin on my arm
a winding reminder

Rachel Barenblat

that I don't need
the addictions of ego
or self-importance.

Every instant
is a new year, a new chance
to bear again in mind

that every sunrise
is the light of creation
in sweet reprise

and every moment
is a prayer I'm blessed
to be able to recite.

Teshuvah

God and I collaborate
on revising the poem of myself.

I decide what needs polishing,
what to preserve and what to lose;

God reads my draft with pursed lips.
If I really mean it, God

sings a new song, one strong
as stone and serene as silk.

I want this year's poem
to be joyful. I want this year's poem

to be measured like flour,
to burn like sweet dry maple.

I want every reader
to come away more certain

that transformation is possible.
I'd like holiness

to fill my words
and my empty spaces.

On Rosh Hashanah it is written
and on Yom Kippur it is sealed:

who will be a haiku and who
a sonnet, who needs meter

Rachel Barenblat

and who free verse, who an epic
and who a single syllable.

If I only get one sound
may it be *yes*, may I be One.

Petition (for *Selichot*)

Compassionate One, remember
we are Your children

help us to know again
that we are cradled

during these awesome days
of changing light

we want to return
to Your lap, to Your arms

remind us how to believe
that we are loved

not for our achievements
but because we are Yours

as the moon of Elul wanes
and the new year rushes in

hear us with compassion
enfold us, don't let us go

Rachel Barenblat

A Prayer for *Tashlich*

Here I am again
ready to let go of my mistakes.

Help me to release myself
from all the ways I've missed the mark.

Help me to stop carrying
the karmic baggage of my poor choices.

As I cast this bread upon the waters
lift my troubles off my shoulders.

Help me to know that last year is over,
washed away like crumbs in the current.

Open my heart to blessing and gratitude.
Renew my soul as the dew renews the grasses.

And we say together:
Amen.

Hineni: **Here I stand**

Here I stand
painfully aware of my flaws
quaking in my shoes
and in my heart.

I'm here on behalf of this *kahal*
though the part of me
that's quick to knock myself
says I'm not worthy to lead them.

All creation was nurtured
in Your compassionate womb!
God of our ancestors, help me
as I call upon your mercy.

Don't blame this community
for the places where I miss the mark
in my actions or my heart
in my thoughts or in our davening.

Each of us is responsible
for her own *teshuvah*.
Help us remember that
without recriminations.

Accept my prayer
as though I were exactly the leader
this community needs in this moment,
as though my voice never faltered.

Free me from my own baggage
that might get in the way.

Rachel Barenblat

See us through the rose-colored glasses
of Your mercy.

Transform our suffering into gladness.
Dear One, may my prayer reach You
wherever You are
for Your name's sake.

All praise is due to You, Dear One
Who hears the prayers of our hearts.

Al Chet Shechatati Lefanecha:
For the sin I have sinned before You

I need to speak these words aloud
and to know that the universe hears them.
I get caught in old patterns and paradigms;
I am stubborn and hard-headed.
In the last year I have missed the mark
more than I want to admit.
Forgive me, Source of all being,
for the sin I have sinned before You

By allowing my body to be an afterthought
too often and too easily;
By not walking, running, leaping, climbing
or dancing although I am able;
By eating in my car and at my desk,
mindlessly and without blessing;
By not embracing those who needed it,
not allowing myself to be embraced;
By not praising every body's beauty,
with our quirks and imperfections.

By letting my emotions run roughshod
over the needs of others;
By poking at sources of hurt
like a child worrying a sore tooth;
By revealing my heart before those
who neither wanted nor needed to see it;
By hiding love, out of fear of rejection,
instead of giving love freely;
By dwelling on what's internal
when the world is desperate for healing.

Rachel Barenblat

By indulging in intellectual argument
without humility or consideration;
By reading words of vitriol,
cultivating hot indignation;
By eschewing intellectual discomfort
that might prod me into growing;
By living in anticipation,
and letting anxiety rule me;
By accepting defeatist thinking
and the comfortable ache of despair.

By not being awake and grateful,
despite uncountable blessings;
By not being sufficiently gentle,
with my actions or with my language;
By being not pliant and flexible,
but obstinate, stark, and unbending;
By not being generous with my time,
with my words or with my being;
By not being kind to everyone
who crosses my wandering path.

For all of these, eternal Source of forgiveness
Help me know myself to be pardoned
Help me feel in my bones that I'm forgiven
Remind me I'm always already at/one with You.

Sukkot
through
Simchat Torah

Prayer Before Building the Sukkah

for the sturdiness of my house
and for the willingness to leave it

for this chance to build
a temporary home, to remember

nomad desert wandering
and harvest houses: thank You.

Connect me, God, with all who labor
here and everywhere.

Increase my compassion
for anyone who has no home.

There is no Temple, and I do not farm:
all I can offer You

is the work of my hands
my heart, open as these walls.

Geshem: Prayer for Rain

Millennia ago, the earth was washed in water
connections sparked unimaginable across the water

the life we know begins cradled in water
each human being emerges in a flood of water

from ancient times we've prayed to God for water
not too much, not too little, just enough water

this year the landscape I first knew lacked water
grasslands parched, thirsting for drops of water

this year the hills where I live ran with water
seeping through roofs, swelling doors shut with water

to mark holy times we immerse ourselves in water
washing our old hurts away in water

in the city of gold, rooftop tanks collect water
those who have and those who lack fight over water

in the beginning, presence hovered over water
mysterious and unknowable like deep water

the bodies we inhabit are made of water
our veins and tissues stay functional through water

we couldn't stand and offer praise without water
source of all, be kind to us: send water.

Rachel Barenblat

A Sukkot Prayer for the Bedouin

Ribbono Shel Olam, Master of the Universe —
Shekhinah, Whose wings shelter creation —

Once our people wandered the desert sands.
Now we merely vacation in rootlessness

While our Bedouin neighbors perch
Without permission, their goats forbidden to graze.

Time after time the bulldozers tear down homes
And playgrounds, uprooting spindly olive trees

To make room for someone else's future forest,
As though saplings mattered more than children.

As we sit beneath palm fronds, corn stalks, pine boughs
Decked with gourds and strings of lights, as we

Invite our nomadic ancestors to join us
For tea and conversation, help us, God

To feel the suffering of every Bedouin parent
Whose children wake from demolition nightmares;

To recognize the merit in their love
Of living lightly on the land.

Once, our Temple — God's sukkah, a house
Of prayer for all peoples — was razed by hate.

Holy One of Blessing, move us now to protect
Those who live in temporary circumstance

Which is all of us who dwell on earth.
Help our hands and hearts to bring repair.

Hoshanna Rabbah Prayer

My footsteps across
this patch of earth's scalp
release the scent of thyme.

Even in the rain
the squirrels have been busy
denuding the corncobs.

The wind has dangled
my autumn garlands. I untangle
them one last time.

Every day the sukkah becomes
more a sketch of itself.
The canvas walls dip

and drape, the cornstalks
wither, revealing more
of the variegated sky.

Today we ask: God, please save
this ark and all that it holds.
Today the penultimate taste

of honey on our bread.
Today we beat willow branches
until the leaves fall.

The end of this long walk
through fasts and feasts:
we're footsore, hearts weary

from pumping emotion. We yearn
to burrow into the soil
and close our eyes. We won't know

what's been planted in us
until the sting of horseradish
pulls us forth into freedom.

Meditation for *Shemini Atzeret*

From the heights of Yom Kippur we fall
into the embrace of a world that shakes,
structures so airy and light
they don't hide the autumn gold
of Berkshire hills, the white press of sky.
Funny to think of dwelling in this house:

hardly enough wall to call it a house,
these two-by-fours we hope won't fall,
roof of cornstalks open to the sky
rattling when the wind makes them shake.
Around me the trees are strung tinsel-gold.
I inhabit bright blocks of light.

After these holidays my soul feels light.
I asked to dwell in God's house
all the days of my life; received gold
fields shorn to stubble, apples fallen
sweet when the trunk gets a shake.
Always perfect, always changing, the sky

rolls back day before darkness, sky
over this little house bedecked with light.
I gather willow, myrtle, palm; shake
them clasped with etrog, the house
for that tiny nugget of tart fall
wrapped in nubbly fragrant gold.

It's the eighth day of festival. I shake
to think of God pleading "don't go." Golden
is our time together in this house,
talking face-to-face beneath the sky.

My tallit skirts my shoulders, light
as cornsilk. The leaves fall

as birch and maple shake.
Time to ask for rain from the desert sky,
changing our prayers with the city of gold
where the limestone pinks with early light,
where once upon a time we built God's house
and learned all things must fall.

I shake my lulav beneath the cloudy sky,
bless the One Who creates this gold light
Whose house is in my heart this fall.

Rachel Barenblat

Mobius
for Simchat Torah

I want to write the Torah
on a mobius strip of parchment

so that the very last lines
(never again will there arise,

arpeggio of signs and wonders
stout strength and subtle teaching)

would lead seamlessly to
the beginning of heavens

and earth, the waters
all wild and waste, and God

hovering over the face of creation
like a mother bird.

This is the strong sinew
that stitches our years together:

that we never have to bear
the heartbreak of the story ending

each year the words are the same
but something in us is different

on a mobius strip of parchment
I want to write the Torah

Pesach to Shavuot

Nisan: Changing
before Pesach

This is a story about change.
Look: the seas are parting.
It's happening now. Open your eyes.

We were slaves to a Pharaoh in Egypt
but God brought us out of there.
This is a story about change.

The womb which had kept us alive
became constricting.
It's happening now. Open your eyes.

It's time to forget our anxieties
and leap off the precipice.
This is a story about change.

Even God is all about change —
I Am Becoming Who I Am Becoming.
It's happening now. Open your eyes.

The moon is almost full
to light our wanderings.
This is a story about change.
It's happening now. Open your eyes.

Meditation on removing leaven
the night before *Pesach*

What does it mean to remove *chametz*
when my cupboard overflows
with toddler-friendly goldfish
and mini-muffins? If there is

any *chametz* I do not know about
— odds are good there are stale O's
in the crevices of the car seat,
but the rest of our leaven is

in plain sight, soft whole-wheat
awaiting jam's unfurling —
that I have not seen or removed,
I disown it. That part

of the formula at least still works.
An invisible line: between
his english muffins, his toasted bread
and my boxes of matzah, waiting.

Even if I don't light a candle
Ribbono shel Olam, help me
to sweep the crumbs from even
the ill-tended corners of my heart.

The too-sour puffery of ego,
the impulse in me that needs
to be in charge, needs to be right,
needs to be praised. The part of me

that forgets the daily importance
of prayer and kindness. I disown it.

Rachel Barenblat

I declare it to be nothing
as ownerless as the dust of the earth.

Freedom
for *Pesach;* in remembrance of the Arab Spring

Liberation comes when people gather
by the tens and by the thousands

demanding that the despot who's held the reins
step down, and in between the slogans

they dish out lentils cooked over open flame,
and homes open up so the protestors can shower

and members of one faith link hands
to protect members of another faith at prayer.

Liberation comes at a cost: not only
the horses and chariots swept away, but

innocents gunned down by their own army,
panicked children lost in the roiling crowds

activists imprisoned for speaking freely,
and when the world stops watching

they may be beaten — or worse.
It's upon us to at least pay attention

on mobile phones and computer screens
as real people rise up to say

we have the right to congregate and to speak
we will not be silenced, we are not afraid.

Rachel Barenblat

Order

Breakfast on kosher macaroons and Diet Pepsi
in the car on the way to Price Chopper for lamb.

Peel five pounds of onions and let the Cuisinart
shred them while you push them down and weep.

Call your mother because you know she's preparing
too, because you want to ask again whether she cooks

matzah balls in salted water or broth, because you can.
Crumble boullion cubes like clumps of wet sand.

Remember the precise mixing order, beating
then stirring then folding, so that for one moment

you can become your grandfather.
Remember the year he taught you this trick

not the year his wife died scant weeks before seder
and he was already befuddled when you came home.

Realize that no matter how many you buy
there are never quite enough eggs at Pesach

especially if you need twelve for the kugel
and eighteen for the kneidlach and another dozen

to hardboil and dip in bowls of stylized tears.
Know you are free! What loss. What rejoicing.

Meditation on Counting the *Omer*

We mark the Omer day
by day, spring unfolding light
as snowflakes in the breeze. One
follows another; we measure each week
of this dusty journey through
wild unknowing. Come and count.

Time to make our qualities count.
The kaleidoscope shifts every day,
each dawn a lens that God shines through.
What in me will be revealed as light
streams into me each week?
Seven colors of the rainbow make one

beam of white. God is One
and God's in everything we count.
Lovingkindness permeates the first week,
then boundaries, harmony, each day
a different lens for light
to warm our hearts as it glows through.

And when the Omer count is through?
We'll stand at Sinai, every one
— every soul that's ever been — light
as Chagall's floating angels. Count
with me, and treasure each day.
A holy pause caps every week.

Endurance comes into play: week
four. We wonder, will we make it through?
Humility and splendor in a single day,
two opposites folded into one.
Roots strengthen us as we count.

Rachel Barenblat

Every day, more work to do and stronger light.

Torah is black fire on white, light
of our lives. In the seventh week
time warps and ripples as we count.
Kingship and presence come through,
transcendence and immanence bundled as one,
wholly revealed on the forty-ninth day...

Feel the light now pouring through.
Each week the seven sefirot become one.
It's time to count the Omer, now, today.

Longing (for Shavuot)

I'm thirsty for davening
in this gritty desert
of car wrecks and cell phones.
Every person killed
anywhere
keeps the promised land
blocked to our passage.

Who knows the path
to short-circuit
this wandering?
Some days manna falls
but others we're back
to toil, scratching
like chickens in the dirt.

If I was there at Sinai
to sign the ketubah
God offered, black fire
on white, most days
I don't remember.
Everyone forgets the unity
we started with.

This year
when our anniversary comes,
God, I want to stay up
all night
to feel the letters
traveling up my hands
into my heart.

Rachel Barenblat

Help me be awake
to Your presence.
I want to sing holy at dawn
with the birds
in the willow behind shul
who open and close each day
with praise.

Grieving
the Broken World

Prayer for the Children of Abraham / Ibrahim
for Israel and Palestine

For every aspiring ballerina huddled
scared in a basement bomb shelter

> *For every toddler in his mother's arms*
> *behind rubble of concrete and rebar*

For every child who's learned to distinguish
"our" bombs from "their" bombs by sound

> *For everyone wounded, cowering, frightened*
> *and everyone furious, planning for vengeance*

For the ones who are tasked with firing shells
where there are grandmothers and infants

> *For the ones who fix a rocket's parabola*
> *toward children on school playgrounds*

For every official who sees shelling Gaza
as a matter of "cutting the grass"

> *And every official who approves launching projectiles*
> *from behind preschools or prayer places*

For every kid taught to lob a bomb with pride
And every kid sickened by explosions

> *For every teenager who considers*
> *"martyrdom" his best hope for a future:*

May the God of compassion and the God of mercy
God of justice and God of forgiveness

God Who shaped creation in Her tender womb
and nurses us each day with blessing

God Who suffers the anxiety and pain
of each of His unique children

God Who yearns for us to take up
the work of perfecting creation

God Who is reflected in those who fight
and in those who bandage the bleeding —

May our Father, Mother, Beloved, Creator
cradle every hurting heart in caring hands.

Soon may we hear in the hills of Judah
and the streets of Jerusalem

in the olive groves of the West Bank
and the apartment blocks of Gaza City

in the kibbutz fields of the Negev
and the neighborhoods of Nablus

the voice of fighters who have traded weapons
for books and ploughs and bread ovens

the voice of children on swings and on slides
singing nonsense songs, unafraid

the voice of reconciliation and new beginnings
in our day, speedily and soon.

And let us say:
amen.

Rachel Barenblat

God, Let Me Cry On Your Shoulder
after the Newtown shootings

God, let me cry on Your shoulder.
Rock me like a colicky baby.
Promise me You won't forget

each of Your perfect reflections
killed today. Promise me
You won't let me forget, either.

I'm hollow, stricken like a bell.
Make of my emptiness a channel
for Your boundless compassion.

Soothe the children who witnessed
things no child should see,
the teachers who tried to protect them

but couldn't, the parents
who are torn apart with grief,
who will never kiss their beloveds again.

Strengthen the hands and hearts
of Your servants tasked with caring
for those wounded in body and spirit.

Help us to find meaning
in the tiny lights we kindle tonight.
Help us to trust

that our reserves of hope
and healing are enough
to carry us through.

We are Your hands: put us to work.
Ignite in us the unquenchable yearning
to reshape our world

so that violence against children
never happens again, anywhere.
We are Your grieving heart.

Rachel Barenblat

Prayer After the Bombing

after the Boston Marathon attack

Plant your feet firmly on the ground, your head
held high as though by a string.

Listen to the red-winged blackbirds, the spring frogs.
There is an aquifer in your heart: send a dipper down.

What have you drawn forth? Send it
out of this room like waves of song.

Float it around the Hairpin Turn, along
the old Mohawk Trail. Direct it toward the rising sun.

Our hearts are in the east though we are in the west.
Blanket the wounded city with melody.

Sing to the runners with aching hamstrings
to the bewildered families who lined the marathon route

to the children who are trying to make sense
to the adults who are trying to make sense

to the EMTs and policemen who ran
not away from the suffering, but into the fire

sing to the grieving families, here and everywhere.
Inhale again, reach into your well:

is there light even for the twisted soul of the bomber?
Now sing to yourself, sluice your own wounds.

We are loved by an unending love.
Listen to the birds again, and remember.

Psalm for the Three Weeks

It is easy to offer praises
when all the world is green
and gold, when the thrush
trails off and on, at ease,
for long sweet minutes.

Oak and birch and maple
once ravaged by caterpillars
have grown new leaves,
pale like spring
through the crescent moon

now waning will take us
through Av, through August,
days that loll like lions.
I don't want to remember
destruction, I want to skip

ahead to the birthday
of the gleaming world
and ignore the way that
anyone has ever felt
disowned or distant or alone.

But if I forget the losses
of my friends in the places
we call home and holy
may my poems dry up
like an empty creekbed.

Rachel Barenblat

Prayer for Syria

Shekhinah, in Whose womb creation is nurtured:
when your children are slaughtered you weep.

Bring peace beneath Your fierce embrace
to Syria. Let a new image of the world be born

in which American Jews pray for Syrians, who pray
for Israelis, who pray for Palestinians, who pray

even for American Jews. Fill the hearts
of the insurgents with Your compassion

so that when the old regime comes to its end
no one seeks the harsh justice of retaliation.

Awaken conscience in the Syrian government
and spark their dormant mercy. And for us:

help us to wield our power in service of good
and strengthen our resolve not to turn away.

We bless You, Source of Mercy. Bring wholeness
to this broken creation. And let us say: Amen.

As Tisha b'Av Approaches

We begin our descent
toward the rubble.

Our hearts crack open
and sorrow comes flooding in.

Help us to believe
that tears can transform,

that redemption is possible.
The walls will come down:

open our eyes, give us strength
not to look away.

Rachel Barenblat

After the Fall (Tisha b'Av)

The Mishna says
senseless hatred
knocked the Temple down

not the Romans with their siege engines —
or not only them, but
our ancestors too

who slipped into petty backbiting
ignored Shabbat
forgot how to offer their hearts

we're no better
we who secretly know we're right
holier-than-they

we who roll our eyes
and patronize, who check email
even on the holiest of days

who forget that
a prayer is more than a tune
more than words on a page

after every shooting parents weep
and we're too busy arguing
motive to comfort them

across the Middle East parents weep
and we're too busy arguing
borders to comfort them

in our nursing homes parents weep
shuddering and alone
and we're too busy —

even now what sanctuaries
what human hearts
are damaged and burned

while we snipe at each other
or insist we're not responsible
or avert our gaze?

Psalms

My Psalm 151

I have learned to see Your voice
in ink on parchment
words filligreed with crowns
holy interpretations sparking forth

help me, God
to hear Your voice echoing
through the vocal chords of those
who sit on my couch

help me find You in the lives
of my beloved friends; help me find You
in the bitter alongside the sweet
and to name You there

I yearn to offer the question
which will make Your presence
suddenly, delightfully
manifest

like the warmth
of a fire kindled against the damp
or the joy of unexpected music
resonating deep in our bones

Six psalms of praise: *Hallel*

1. (113)

Yesterday's sleet has melted: I offer praise
the sky is a perfect eggshell: I offer praise

my husband has taken the baby out of the house
freeing me to wrap myself in rainbow silk

to squint into the sun and sing psalms
I offer praise

2. (114)

let all offer praise
to what brings us forth from constriction
when we remember to say thank you
the hills and horizon dance

3. (115)

You spun the heavens on Your unthinkable loom
and fashioned the elements of creation with Your deft hands

the heavens are Yours
but the earth is in our keeping

the dead can't praise, but we can
help us remember

Rachel Barenblat

4. (116)

I yearn to serve
as my ancestors yearned to serve

you have loosened
the cords around my heart

5. (117)

let every nation wake up, seized
by the yearning to praise

help us manifest mercy and truth
both are Yours

6. (118)

let gratitude well up like water
    lovingkindness is forever
let my community call forth
    lovingkindness is forever
let all who marry fear and awe call forth
    lovingkindness is forever

from the straits of depression I have called out
You answer me with heart wide as the fields

open Your gates for me
I yearn to enter and give thanks

help me know that what was rejected in me
is cornerstone for something new

this day, right here, was shaped by You
I want to rejoice in it

Dear One, bring us salvation
bring us Your help

You give us light; in return we imagine
festival processions, our arms full of branches

bless all who come in Your name
    lovingkindness is forever

Rachel Barenblat

Psalm of the Sky
for those who dwell in uncertainty

You are my parachute
I will not fall

in Your arms I float easy
and the air buoys me

I can do backflips, I can wave
to my fellow skydivers

I can sink into unknowing
without freezing

though I have no idea
how distant the ground

or where I will land
I am not afraid

Your silent presence
comforts me

when You dance with me
I forget to feel ungainly

You will cradle me
all the days of my life

spin with me
in the stratosphere forever

Psalm of Wonder

I boast I grew a baby
from component cells. Big deal:

You built the cosmos
from component atoms, and those

have moving parts which shift,
performing particle or wave.

As photons yearn for the void
my heart yearns for You

though when we meet
I disappear.

When I ascend the ladder
I understand entanglement

though when I fall back down
my human brain can't grasp

the endless *ein-sof*
of Your quantum fields.

for R' Fern Feldman and Dr. Karen Barad

Rachel Barenblat

Winter Psalm

The wind whips spirals of snow
dervishes dancing across icy asphalt

snowplows call out to one another
backing up to ply their routes again

the atmosphere looms, pregnant
with the promise of precipitation

and I? I scatter handfuls of cat litter
across the driveway's uneven terrain

casting prayers for the safe passage
of all who come, and all who go

Seven reasons: Psalm 147

You rebuild your city with our hands
and gather our scattered sparks.
You darn the heels of our hearts
and comfort us with bandages.

You smear sunrise across the heavens
like raspberry jam
and coax every blade of grass
to emerge from the dark comfort of soil.

And you love our fragility
not our particle physics
nor the bridges we labored to plant
across the inlets your glaciers carved.

You lay down ice like glass
and frost like lace on our windowpanes
and then you breathe a January thaw
and our frozen places melt.

Rachel Barenblat

Psalm of Parenthood

Mother of all, remake me
in Your image. Make me as noble
as the daffodils nodding graciously.
Root me in my generations.
Help me hold onto the splendor
my son sees when he runs toward me
at the end of a schoolday.
Give me the flannel-soft patience
for one more board book, one more cartoon.
Help me to balance the scales
of work and child
gentleness and strength.
Reinforce my boundaries
so I never confuse my child's issues
with my own.
Enlarge my ribcage
to encompass this overflowing love.

Shabbat

Preparations
   for Shabbat evening

Breathe deep, from the belly,
as if for singing.
Notice your vertebrae, the curve
where spine tilts to pelvis,
and inhale everything into place.

Blanket the mind
as trees blanket grass with leaves.
Drape woven wool over
every sharp worry and task.
They'll survive a night without you.

Drizzle cornmeal on cookie sheets
like a sand painting
of the chaos in which creation begins.
Let *challah* dough rise and fall
like slow breathing.

Tonight the sky arches
like bent boughs roofed with cloud,
spangled with constellations.
The Breath of Life spreads peace
over creation.

Nishmat Kol Chai: The Breath of All Life
for Shabbat morning

Breath of our bodies
and harmattan of our ambitions

hurricane of our angers
and chinook of our forgiveness

tempest of our childbirths
and cold front of our silences

articulated gasp of pain
and muffled sigh of pleasure

inbreath of my housecat
and outbreath of every tree

gust that reshapes coastlines
and tempest of our hearts

wind of the physical world
and the realms of emanation beyond

Breath of All Life, the breath
of all life blesses Your name.

If every mouth joined right now
in breathing Your praises

if every present thing on earth
stopped so we could laud You

if we all shared the roaring voice
of lion and elephant and walrus,

Rachel Barenblat

the heightened senses
of the mystic and the hunting owl

if we could fly like the Concorde
looping your smoky name across the sky

if we could discard differences: human,
animal, fire, stone, seed, snow

even that cry of togetherness
would not be enough to thank You.

Saturday Afternoon Request

Help me to silence
my mind's aggravation alarm,
to quiet the voice which says
the to-do list matters,
to temporarily eschew
continuous partial attention.

Open me to long slow conversations
on the sunlit grass, to the beat
of the hand-drummers who accompany
the singing of psalms, to a boat
lazily drifting on the glassy surface
of my heart's own pond.

You're waiting for me
like a lover, eager
to embrace me again.
Remind me: this is the way
back to Eden, the bloom
on the thirteen-petaled rose.

Rachel Barenblat

Here and gone
for seudah shlishit, the "third meal" of Shabbat

You're most palpably here
in the moment departure begins.

We turn off the artificial lights,
feel the darkening of the sky.

I'm the deer, caught
in Your presence.

When it grows too dark
we sing without words

and that's what cracks me open.
My cup overflows.

There is nothing but You.
You are everything.

Don't go

Look how the light
is changing. Last night
we waltzed in the doorway,
sang until our voices deepened.

But our time together
is always already ending.
Weekday melodies
peek around the edges.

I'm not ready.
I throw myself at your knees.
What if even our strongest spices
aren't enough to revive me?

I know once we're apart
I'll remember how good it feels
to miss you. How everything
is meant to come and go.

Still, right now
in the light that emanates
from your face, I can imagine
how it would feel

if we didn't need distance
in order to know union
if you didn't need to leave
in order to return.

Rachel Barenblat

Distinctions (Havdalah)
for the end of Shabbat

In the end we're like children:
we thrive on distinctions
between me and you, us and them.
Made in Your image
we separate light from darkness,
family from stranger, weekday
from that fleeting taste of Paradise.

Wax drips from the braided candle.
Cinnamon tingles the nose
to keep us from fainting
as the extra soul departs.
Stop now. Notice this hinge
between Shabbat
and what's next.

Plunge the candle into the wine
but don't cry: even without a flame
our light still shines. This
is our inheritance, better than rubies.
And now it's Saturday night, the cusp
of a new beginning, another day.
This week, may our hearts be whole.

Glossary

Al Chet Shechatati Lefanecha — "for the sin I have sinned
against You;" a first-person variation on a communal
prayer recited on Yom Kippur

Asher yatzar — "You who have formed my body…"

Av — a month on the Hebrew calendar; usually near August

Baruch she'amar — "Blessed is the One Who speaks the
world…"

challah —bread for Shabbat, yeasted, often braided

chametz — leaven

davening — prayer

ein-sof — "without end," the kabbalists' name for limitless
God

Elohai neshama — "My God, the soul You have given me is
pure"

Elul — a month on the Hebrew calendar; before the Days
of Awe

etrog — also known as citron; a nubbly citrus fruit used at
Sukkot

geshem — rain; also the name of a prayer for rain recited on
Shemini Atzeret

Hallel — psalms 113-118, recited on festivals

havdalah — literally "separation; the ceremony which
formally ends Shabbat

Hineni — "Here I am;" also a prayer recited by the prayer-
leader during the Days of Awe

Hoshanna Rabbah — "the great 'Save Us!'" a holiday on the
seventh day of Sukkot

kahal — community

ketubah — marriage contract

kugel — a pudding, usually savory

lulav —palm and willow and myrtle branches, shaken
together with the *etrog* at Sukkot

matzah balls / kneidlach — dumplings made of matzah flour

Mishna — early rabbinic text interpreting the Hebrew Scriptures

neshama — soul / breath

Nishmat kol chai — "The breath of all that lives praises Your name..."

Nisan — a Hebrew month; spring; contains Pesach

Omer — the 49 days between Pesach and Shavuot

Pesach — Passover; remembrance of the Exodus

Ribbono Shel Olam — Master of the Universe

Rosh Hashanah — "the head of the year;" the Jewish New Year

Selichot — a service of penitential prayers recited before and during the Days of Awe

seudah shlishit — the ritual "third meal" of Shabbat; takes place as late afternoon shades toward nightfall on Shabbat

Shabbat — Sabbath

Shavuot — the Feast of Weeks; 50th day after Pesach; celebration of the revelation of the Torah

Shekhinah — one of the kabbalistic names for the immanent Divine Presence, usually conceptualized as feminine

Shemini Atzeret — "The Pause of the Eighth Day;" a minor holiday on the eighth day of Sukkot, when God asks us to linger a little longer

Simchat Torah — Rejoicing in the Torah; a minor holiday on the ninth or tenth day of Sukkot (depending on denomination)

Sukkah — a temporary structure in which we dwell (or at least dine and celebrate) for a week

Sukkot — the name of the fall harvest festival; a remembrance of the Exodus; without a capital letter, this word is the plural of *sukkah*

tallit — prayer shawl

tashlich — the ritual casting-away of our misdeeds on the first day of Rosh Hashanah (enacted by casting bread upon the waters)

Talmud — central post-Biblical text of Rabbinic Judaism

teshuvah — repentance / return / turning-toward-God

Tisha b'Av — the Ninth of Av; day of mourning for the fallen Temples (and, some say, for the brokenness of creation)

tzitzit — fringes which serve as reminders of the commandments

Yom Kippur — the Day of Atonement; ten days after Rosh Hashanah

Acknowledgments

"Asher Yatzar" first appeared in *Zeek* magazine, 2005; it was also published in *God in Your Body* by Jay Michaelson (Jewish Lights, 2006.)

"Psalm for the Three Weeks" first appeared (as "Psalm for Tuesday") in *Brilliant Coroners*, Phoenicia Publishing, 2007.

"Seven reasons (Psalm 147)" first appeared at *The Best American Poetry* blog, December 2008.

"Teshuvah" first appeared in *Chadesh Yameinu*, Congregation Beth Israel, 2008.

"Mobius" first appeared (as "Mobius (V'Zot HaBrakha)") in *70 faces: Torah poems*, Phoenicia Publishing, 2011.

"Without Ceasing" first appeared in *Qarrtsiluni*, the Worship issue, 2011.

"A Sukkot Prayer for the Bedouin" first appeared on the *Rabbis for Human Rights* website, 2012.

"Daily Miracles" and "Prayer After the Bombing" first appeared in *April Daily*, 2013.

"Nissim: Changing," "Baruch She'amar," and "Tele/Presence" first appeared in Soul-Lit: A Journal of Spritual Poetry, 2013

"Meditation on Removing Leaven" first appeared in Soul-Lit, 2014.

"Al Chet Shechatati Lefanecha" first appeared in *Mishkan HaNefesh*, CCAR Press, 2015.

"Freedom" and "Order" first appeared in *The Velveteen Rabbi's Haggadah for Pesach*.

Many of these poems originally appeared, sometimes in earlier forms or with different titles, at the blog Velveteen Rabbi.

Thanks are due to Rabbis Without Borders/Clal for naming me a Rabbis Without Borders Fellow in 2013 and for bringing me into this remarkable community of colleagues.

And thanks to Dale Favier and Cynthia Hoffman, trusted readers and dear friends.

About the Author

Rachel Barenblat holds an MFA from the Bennington Writing Seminars. She was ordained a rabbi by ALEPH: Alliance for Jewish Renewal in 2011. She received a second ordination from ALEPH as a *mashpi'ah ruchanit* (spiritual director) in 2012. Selected as a Rabbis Without Borders Fellow in 2013 by Clal (the Center for Jewish Learning & Leadership), Barenblat serves as co-chair of ALEPH.

Barenblat is author of *70 faces: Torah poems* (Phoenicia Publishing, 2011), *Waiting to Unfold* (Phoenicia Publishing, 2013), and *Open My Lips* (Ben Yehuda Press, 2016) as well as several chapbooks, among them *the skies here* (Pecan Grove Press, 1995), *What Stays* (Bennington Writing Seminars Alumni Chapbook Series, 2002), *chaplainbook* (Laupe House Press, 2006), *See Me*, a chapbook of Elul poems (Velveteen Rabbi Press, 2014), and *Toward Sinai*, a chapbook of Omer poems (Velveteen Rabbi Press, 2015.)

Since 2003 she has blogged as The Velveteen Rabbi, and in 2008 her blog was named one of the top 25 blogs on the internet by TIME. She is perhaps best known for the (free, downloadable) Velveteen Rabbi's *Haggadah for Pesach*, which has been used in homes and synagogues worldwide.

Her poems have appeared in a wide variety of magazines and anthologies, among them *Phoebe*, *The Jewish Women's Literary Annual*, *The Texas Observer*, *The Bloomsbury Anthology of Contemporary Jewish American Poetry* (Bloomsbury, 2013) and *The Poet's Quest For God* (Eyewear Publishing, 2014.)

You can find her prose in *The Women's Seder Sourcebook* (Jewish Lights, 2002), *God: Jewish Choices for Struggling with the Ultimate* (Torah Aura, 2008) and *Keeping Faith in Rabbis: A Community Conversation on Rabbinical Education* (Avenida, 2014) among other places.

She serves Congregation Beth Israel in North Adams, Massachusetts. Find her online at velveteenrabbi.com.

More poetry from
Ben Yehuda Press

from the **Coffee House**
of **Jewish Dreamers**
Poems of Wonder and Wandering

Isidore Century

Abe Mezrich

The House
in the
center of the world
poems from Leviticus and environs

we who
desire

Poems after the Torah

Sue Swartz

from the **Coffee House** of **Jewish Dreamers**

Poems of *Wonder and Wandering*

Isidore Century

"So rich, so full of life, so much *ta'am*, tastiness."
— *Home Planet News*

"FROM THE COFFEE HOUSE OF JEWISH DREAMERS is so rich, so full of life, and has so much *ta'am*, tastiness, that it is almost daunting to review.
   —**Nikki Stiller,** *Home Planet News*

"Isidore Century is a wonderful poet. He writes of traveling to Coney Island; visiting Israel and returning there to the land of Yiddish in which he grew up; his father, who escaped from Poland and made his way illegally to the U.S., where he became an official in the Painter's Union; and about his own reluctant and penetrating faith, 'I keep running from a God/in whom I do not believe/hoping he catches me.'
   —*The New York Jewish Week*

Vayigash
Joseph (3)

I was Joseph's butler and valet,
his only confidant.
He was so busy feeding the whole world
he had no time for friends, or family.
"Your father lives not six days' journey away,"
I told him. "Let me go and inquire after him."
Such a stiff-neck he was, he would not change
his no to not even a maybe.
What did Jacob do, I wondered,
that Joseph should forsake him so?

A famine brought his brothers before him.
"Doth my father yet live?" he asked them.
When told he was,
what weeping and sobbing,
you could hear it all over the palace.
To celebrate, Joseph, who liked to cook,
created *gefilte fish*,
which to this day is served on Friday nights
with red or white horse radish, so strong,
it should make you cry like Joseph and his brothers.

Devarim

What did I have to do with spies?
I was only a kid.
It was my father and mother.
They bet on a sure thing and lost to God.
He sentenced them and an entire generation of losers
to die in the wilderness,
perhaps, if you were lucky, before,
but not one minute more,
than forty years.

We marched, we camped, we prayed.
Day after day, a cloud,
night after night, a fire.
It was so boring some of us wanted to return to Egypt.
But Moses had a revelation:
you will not find it in any *midrash*:
he made up a game, two teams,
eleven men on a side,
who took turns trying to kick a large round ball
through the goal posts of the other team.
It was tribe against tribe.
If Moses wasn't the referee, bloodshed.
We were saved from boredom but not from each other.

When the last of the generation of the spies died,
we arrived at the Moab Mountains,
below, the River Jordan;
beyond, like a misty dream
waiting for us to dream it,
the Promised Land.
I wanted to run down the mountainside
and leap into the waters
but I couldn't swim.
I asked Moses to teach me;
he couldn't swim either,

He had a chance to learn when he was a Prince of Egypt,
but was afraid of the great Nile crocodile.
And now there was no time to learn,
he had to prepare a farewell speech.
It was always something with him:
Pharaoh, Sinai, the Golden Calf, the Spies;
he never found a minute to enjoy himself.
Maybe if he had a hobby,
like bird watching or pottery,
the Torah would have had some cheerful stories
or a few good Israelite jokes between the verses
 of Six Hundred and Thirteen mitzvot.

Bananas

My high school girlfriend Milly Aronow used to make
me banana sandwiches. A chubby five foot two, with eyes
not of blue, but grey, like a cloud that has its own reasons
for going where it's going. She wore her shiny, dark hair in
bangs. It gave her a cute, innocent look. But innocent she
was not. She had a saucy turn of lips and a teasing, knowing
air as though she knew all about sex but wouldn't tell you
all she knew. And she knew a lot. At fifteen she could talk
convincingly about condoms, diaphragms, periods and
deviate sexual behavior. She even knew an abortionist, "just
in case," she would say. But there was never any just in case
with Milly. Necking was as far as she went.

I used to take her to the movies Saturdays. On Tuesdays
and Fridays, when her mother was doing an afternoon shift
selling dishes at Woolworths, we would neck, listen to music
on the radio and eat banana sandwiches. Sometimes, onion
or cucumber. She had shown me photos which showed
her wearing jodpurs and holding the reins of a horse at her
father's estate in New Jersey. That made me think she was
well off and banana sandwiches were kind of neat.

Now, as I look back at those afternoons, I see things
differently. I see how old the sofa bed she slept in was, the
cracked dishes, the rug that was shabby and the blouses and
dresses she wore that had been washed and pressed so many
times they were as thin as paper. I used to think she stole
school supplies for the fun of it, not because she hadn't the
money to buy them. She was poor, poorer than me. And I
could kick myself for not taking her to the Loew's Paradise
as I had promised.

Promises, promises. If you don't keep them they're like
banana peels which you will step on someday and fall flat on
your remorse.

Abe Mezrich

The House
in the
center of the world
poems from Leviticus and environs

Each installment of Abe's still, small voice is a miniature jewel, poetically illuminating with its delicate facets otherwise hidden elements of each parsha.
Dan Friedman, managing editor, *The Forward*

These poems remind us that our Creator is forgiving, that the spiritual and physical can inform one another, and that the supernatural can be carried into the everyday.
Yehoshua November, author of *God's Optimism*

How pure do you need to be?

There is a water basin in the courtyard to God's Tent.
It stands between the altar and the Tent itself.
The priests purify their hands from it
and purify their feet from it
before they approach the altar
or before they enter the Tent.
*

They enter God's courtyard
hands unwashed
and feet unwashed.
They wash their hands
right there, beside God's altar,
before His Tent.
*

So, perhaps
you need to be clean and pure
to serve before God.

But to walk toward Him,
you only need to be ready
to wash yourself.

Exodus 30:17-21

When you matter

i
God speaks
of the man who brings a sacrifice
in God's holy Tent:
how he lays hands on the animal
and slaughters it before God.
And God speaks
of how after the priests sprinkle the animal blood
and prepare the animal parts
they must set the fire on the altar
and lay wood on the fire
and lay the animal on the fire.

ii
First comes the man
who comes to God.
Then comes the priest
with God's fire.
*
This is the opposite
of the Creation of the world,
that begins with God's Light
and culminates in Man.
Here, it is a person
who triggers God's flame.

iii
Here is the amazing dialogue:
Our world begins with God's Light;
when we come to God
we let God's Light begin.

Leviticus 1:1-9

I have read this according to the simple reading of the passage, but the Halakha is clear that the flame is constantly on the altar. See Leviticus 6:5-7 and Maimonides Temidin Umusafin Chapter 2.

we who
desire

Poems and Torah riffs

Sue Swartz

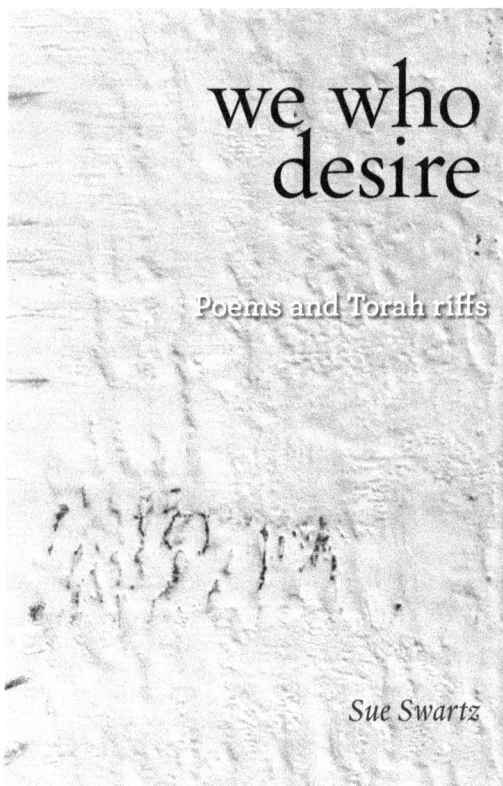

"Sue Swartz does magnificent acrobatics with the Torah in *We Who Desire*. She takes the English that's become staid and boring, and adds something that's new and strange and exciting. These are poems that leave a taste in your mouth, and you walk away from them thinking, what did I just read? Oh, yeah. It's the Bible.
—Matthue Roth, author, *Yom Kippur A Go-Go, Never Mind the Goldbergs, My First Kafka*

CREATION

Like a pencil poised for calculation, a key not yet turned
in the twitchy ignition, so was the curved throat of God
in the nothing before the ready,
                                   so ready, beginning.

Then: Big Bang. Black letters proclaimed onto white
parchment universe—

Water swirling away from water. Sapphire sky
pouring through. Crackling horizon, pulsing light—

Seeds sprouting into fruit, into trees ripe with the will-be—

Whirling serpents and creepers of the soil; swarming,
leaping, winged things—

And last to come, dusty youngsters made in the image
            (haploid or diploid, twin & twin)—

Each particle & personality called into itself by a voice.

That voice. Insistent, unfurling. The deafening pulse
of now:
                                   so good.

(the book of women)

This is the book of women—

In it, the body's fruit is legal tender.
In it, sons are made in the image of stranger,
master, lover, king.

Status is earned between the thighs.

Also, this is the book of virile possessions
       (flocks
       servants
       wives).

And the book of volatile love.
In it, put out and put up with.

In it, sisterly deception and desperate measures.
       All those mandrakes!
       All those fancy push-up bras!

❦

In it, gathering flowers in broad daylight.
In it: parking lot, backyard, Tuesday night date.

Where brother, stranger, husband.
Where alcohol, opportunity, tithe of war.

Also, this is the book of he said, she said.

And the book of failure to report.
        None of it happened.
        Or maybe every last detail.

In it, men hold on to what is theirs.
Force and tenderness is found on every page.

Read between the lines—
        There's a woman telling her story.

❧

When pleasure is spoken of in past tense—
When your selves do not add up—
Your wife calls you by another name—
Your brother loves you after all—
When your babies grow into women you cannot corral,
        men with steel in their hands—
When more has been taken than you have left—
You have arrived at the nub of your story.

❧

virility duplicity
all that comes to pass

everything begot
begets its opposite

message you cannot elude
gifts you cannot parse

all you are
in relation to the other

❦

This is the book of sorrow.

In it, Rachel weeping for her children.
It in, grief plentiful as grains of sand.

As stars in the sky.

In it, the 14-year-old girl who—
The boy sitting next to her when—

All that is born from the body's fruit,
wrestling with what names us.

Ceasing to be coming to be.

THESE ARE THE WORDS

1.

This is the book of sayings and things,
what is made real by our telling.

In it: our story is   story.
In it: allusion we cannot grasp.

And this is the book of incidents & accidents,
where God came in person to say—

Where floating out there, tumbling
down there—

Where repetition raises an arc of desire
and we spiral back—

2.

We were nothing at first.
Then the story found us.

We were young once—

Dust before we were multitudes.
Blueprint before we were steel.

Every \stôr-ē\ is like this story:
part rousing prophecy, part iron furnace.

3.

I am an experiment.
I am a recipient.

Preview: Sue Swartz

Preservationist. Translator. Monument.
I remember it though I was not there.
Saw it with my own eyes.
I am a mnemonic.
I am a mosaic. Off-key chorale.

I am a time machine.
I am a telegraph tapping
          from my mouth to your ear—
History, taxonomy, fragment, reprise.
Does it matter if the words are true
or truth or truer still?

I am a schematic.
I am a joist.
Bastard vernacular. Everything begot.
I am revelation and bad relation,
an encyclopedia of this and that.
Both/and. Either/or.
Enclosure, torment, skeleton, key.

I am a reader.
I am the text.

On my knees in the paper temple.

4.

This is the book of annotation.

In it, we rewrite the way back.
In it, we wander out loud—

Each of us a syllable trying
to understand.